T0020144

TABLE OF CONTENTS

Words in **bold** are in the glossary.

CLOTHING AROUND THE WORLD

Clothes are more than just fabric. They tell a story. Clothing can tell where you live. It can tell what job you have. Clothing can also tell the set of beliefs you have. What kind of story do your clothes tell?

Traditional dress in Ukraine

A family living in Siberia, Russia

In some places, people dress the same. Some people only wear **traditional** clothes. Others wear the latest fashion.

Many people dress for the **weather**. They may live where it's cold, hot, or wet.

DRESSING FOR THE WEATHER

What do you wear in the winter? People wear certain clothes for types of weather. They bundle up in very cold places.

Mongolian winters get very cold. There people wear long, thick robes. The robes are called deels. Bright colors shine on the outside of deels. Sheep or goat hair keeps the inside warm. People wear fur hats and **felt**-lined boots.

A Mongolian woman

A Sami man

In Finland, the Sami people herd reindeer. It snows there. They wear high-collared coats. The coats have bright patterns. Women wear long skirts under the coats. Men wear pants. They all put on hats and boots.

Some parts of the world get very hot. People wear loose, light clothes to stay cool.

Women in India wear **saris**. They wrap fabric around a shirt and pants. It makes a skirt. The rest of the fabric drapes over the shoulder.

Indian women dressed in saris

A Cameroon mother and child

People in Cameroon wear light fabric too. Women wear dresses and skirts with many colors. Their clothes are loose. This keeps them cool on hot days.

DRESSING FOR THE JOB

People around the world have clothes they must wear to work. These are called **uniforms**. Some clothes protect workers. Doctors wear gloves and masks. These protect doctors from germs. Firefighters' clothes protect them from fire.

A teacher wearing a gho

Some jobs have dress codes. Men in the government in Bhutan have uniforms. They must wear a gown called a gho. The gown is knee length. It's tied at the waist. Higher ranking men wear a colored cloth across their bodies.

Ranchers in the U.S. often ride horses. They herd cows. They wear cowboy hats. The hats shade their eyes from the sun. They wear tall boots. They wear jeans that last a long time. Many use flannel shirts to keep warm. Or they roll up the sleeves to keep cool.

TRADITIONAL DRESS

Some clothing styles haven't changed for hundreds of years. Some people wear traditional clothing every day. Others wear it only on special days.

Some men in Germany wear leather shorts. The shorts are called *lederhosen* (LAY-dur-ho-zuhn). Leather **suspenders** hold them up. Men wear these shorts on holidays such as Oktoberfest. Some farmers wear lederhosen while they work.

In Scotland, people wear skirts called kilts. The skirts are made of wool. They have crisscross patterns.

Each family has its own pattern. They can wear kilts for events such as weddings. Men and boys wear kilts when they play sports.

A Scottish man wearing a kilt

A Japanese couple wearing kimonos

Men and women in Japan wear long robes called *kimonos* (kih-MOH-nohs). The fabric has patterns or pictures. Women wear bright kimonos. Men wear dark ones. Some people wear them every day. Others wear them only for holidays or when they dress up.

Women in Ecuador wear long, **woven** rectangles over their shoulders. They wear it with a skirt and a hat. Men wear a woven **poncho**. They wear it with pants and a hat.

Some people in Australia wear felt hats, tall boots, and long raincoats. This is called bush wear. It's good for hiking in the outdoors.

DRESSING FOR GROUPS

People like to wear clothing to show what group they are in. Some clothes show **cultures**. Culture is a person's beliefs, **customs**, and way of life. Some clothes are only for men. Some are only for women. Some clothes are for certain ages.

People of the Zulu tribe in South Africa change their style. Men wear animal skins at their waist called aprons. Young men wear knee-length aprons. Older men wear aprons that go to the ground.

Zulu women wear clothes to show if they're married. Young women wear short skirts. Each skirt has many colors. After they get married, they cover up in a long black cape.

Many groups and villages have certain clothing. The Hmong of China also wear certain colors and patterns. Their clothes show the Black, White, Striped, and Flower tribes of Hmong. The Flower tribe wears the brightest clothes. The Black tribe wears all black.

HEAD COVERINGS

People all over the world wear hats. Some people wear hats because of their **religion**. They follow a set of rules based on their beliefs. Others put on special hats just for holidays.

Some Jewish men wear a small cap that covers part of the head.

A Vietnamese farmer

People in Vietnam wear big palm-leaf hats. This type of hat is called a *non la* (NUHN LAH). Men, women, and children wear them. The hats protect them from the hot sun and rain. They can use the hats to carry things.

In Iran, Muslim women wear head scarves. They cover their heads for their religion. The scarves often have colors that match their clothes.

For some holidays, French people wear traditional hats. Women wear tall lace headdresses. Their hair is up under the hats. Men wear flat hats. They are called berets. Some have badges on them. Soldiers also wear berets.

People do not always wear clothes that tell about their culture. Many people around the world now wear jeans and T-shirts. But most people still use clothes to say something about who they are. What story do your clothes tell?

A mall in Japan

MAP

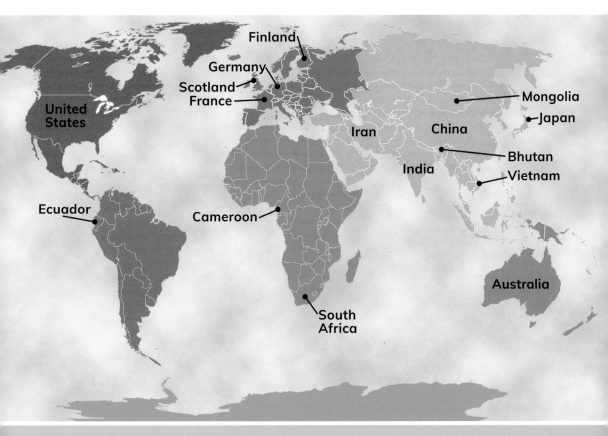

Around the world people wear different clothes. See which places were talked about in this book!

GLOSSARY

culture (KUHL-chur)—a group of people's beliefs, customs, and way of life

custom (KUHS-tuhm)—the usual way of doing something for a group of people

felt (FELT)—a type of smooth cloth usually made from wool

poncho (PON-choh)—a cloak that looks like a blanket with a hole in the center from the head; ponchos were originally worn in South America

religion (ri-LIJ-uhn)—a set of spiritual beliefs that people follow

sari (SAH-ree)—a long piece of cloth that is wrapped around a woman's body

suspender (suh-SPEN-dur)—one of two supporting bands of fabric worn across the shoulders and clasp at the waistband of pants, shorts, or skirts

traditional (truh-DISH-uhn-uhl)—passed down through time

uniform (YOO-nih-FORM)—special clothes that members of a particular group wear

weather (WEH-thur)—the condition outdoors; weather changes with each season

woven (WOH-vin)—being made of thread, yarn, or strips of material that are laced together

READ MORE

Britton, Arthur K. *Native American Clothing: From Moccasins to Mukluks*. New York: Gareth Stevens Publishing, 2018.

Murphy, Charles. *Clothing Around the World*. New York: Gareth Stevens Publishing, 2017.

Weston, Margeaux. *Clothing Inspired by Nature*. North Mankato, MN: Capstone Press, 2020.

INTERNET SITES

Traditional Japanese Clothing
www.education.com/worksheet/article/traditional-japanese-clothing/?source=related_materials&order=6

Wedding Dresses Across Asia
www.youtube.com/watch?v=DVahZ5NaxCo

Around the World Dress Up
www.girlgames.com/around-the-world-dress-up.html

INDEX